CHECKERBOARD BIOGRAPHY LIBRARY

U.S. PRESIDENTS

The
United States Presidents

BILL CLINTON

ABDO Publishing Company

BreAnn Rumsch

visit us at
www.abdopublishing.com

Published by ABDO Publishing Company, 8000 West 78th Street, Edina, Minnesota 55439.
Copyright © 2009 by Abdo Consulting Group, Inc. International copyrights reserved in all
countries. No part of this book may be reproduced in any form without written permission from the
publisher. The Checkerboard Library™ is a trademark and logo of ABDO Publishing Company.

Printed in the United States, North Mankato, Minnesota.

Cover Photo: Getty Images
Interior Photos: Alamy pp. 8, 11, 28; AP Images pp. 13, 15, 16, 18, 19, 20, 22, 24, 26, 27;
    Corbis pp. 9, 10, 12; Getty Images pp. 5, 17, 21, 25, 29; iStockphoto p. 32

Editor: Heidi M.D. Elston
Art Direction & Cover Design: Neil Klinepier
Interior Design: Neil Klinepier

Library of Congress Cataloging-in-Publication Data

Rumsch, BreAnn, 1981-
  Bill Clinton / BreAnn Rumsch.
    p. cm. -- (The United States presidents)
  Includes bibliographical references and index.
  ISBN 978-1-60453-447-4
  1. Clinton, Bill, 1946---Juvenile literature. 2. Presidents--United States--Biography--Juvenile
literature. I. Title.
  E886.R86 2009
  973.929092--dc22
  [B]
                              2008037173
012009
062010

CONTENTS

BILL CLINTON

Bill Clinton was the forty-second president of the United States. His interest in politics began at a young age. In high school, he participated in government clubs. Then in college, he served as class president.

After college, Clinton taught law school. Then, he was elected **attorney general** of Arkansas. Clinton later served five terms as governor of Arkansas.

In 1993, Clinton became president. As president, he worked hard to improve the **economy**. Clinton also helped make peace in other nations.

President Clinton's popularity won him a second term. Yet, he faced personal **scandals** that led to his **impeachment** in 1998. Still, he continued to work hard for Americans.

After leaving the White House, Clinton remained active in many worthy causes. He started the William J. Clinton Foundation in 2002. Then in 2004, he opened the William J. Clinton Presidential Center.

Bill Clinton

TIMELINE

1946 - On August 19, William Jefferson Clinton was born in Hope, Arkansas.

1963 - Clinton became interested in a political career after meeting President John F. Kennedy.

1968 - Clinton graduated from Georgetown University in Washington, D.C.

1973 - Clinton graduated from Yale Law School in New Haven, Connecticut.

1975 - On October 11, Clinton married Hillary Diane Rodham.

1976 - Clinton was elected attorney general of Arkansas.

1979 - Clinton became governor of Arkansas.

1982 - Clinton was reelected governor; he went on to win the next three elections in a row.

1993 - On January 20, Clinton became the forty-second U.S. president; Congress passed the Brady Handgun Violence Prevention Act and the Family and Medical Leave Act.

1994 - On January 1, the North American Free Trade Agreement took effect; Kenneth Starr began investigating the Whitewater affair.

1996 - President Clinton was elected to a second term.

1998 - The U.S. House of Representatives impeached Clinton in December.

1999 - On February 12, the U.S. Senate found Clinton not guilty.

2002 - Clinton started the William J. Clinton Foundation.

2004 - Clinton published his autobiography called *My Life*; in December, the William J. Clinton Presidential Center opened in Little Rock, Arkansas.

2007 - Clinton published the book *Giving: How Each of Us Can Change the World*.

DID YOU KNOW?

Bill Clinton enjoys many hobbies. He stays active by jogging and golfing. He also likes to read, solve crossword puzzles, and play the tenor saxophone.

Inaugurated at age 46, Clinton became the third-youngest person to serve as U.S. president. John F. Kennedy and Theodore Roosevelt were younger when they were inaugurated. Kennedy was 43 and Roosevelt was just 42.

In 1996, Clinton became the first Democratic president reelected in 60 years. Back in 1936, Democrat Franklin D. Roosevelt was elected to his second of four terms.

In 2000, Clinton appointed Norman Mineta secretary of commerce. Mineta was the first Asian American to serve in a U.S. president's cabinet.

PRESIDENT OF THE
POTUS
UNITED STATES

EARLY YEARS

William Jefferson Clinton was born on August 19, 1946, in Hope, Arkansas. He was called Billy when he was young. Billy's mother, Virginia Dell Blythe, named him William Jefferson Blythe III after his father. His father had died in a car

Billy's childhood home in Hope, Arkansas

accident three months before Billy was born.

When Billy was two, his mother moved to New Orleans, Louisiana, to attend nursing school. Virginia left Billy in Hope. He stayed with her parents, Eldridge and Edith Cassidy. Billy's grandparents ran a grocery store in Hope. They took good care of Billy.

FAST FACTS

BORN - August 19, 1946
WIFE - Hillary Diane Rodham
    (1947–)
CHILDREN - 1
POLITICAL PARTY - Democrat
AGE AT INAUGURATION - 46
YEARS SERVED - 1993–2001
VICE PRESIDENT - Al Gore

8

They also taught him to count and read. Growing up, Billy especially liked reading about Native Americans.

Virginia returned to Hope when Billy was four. Shortly after, she married a car dealer

Billy (left)*, his mother, and his brother, Roger*

named Roger Clinton. In 1953, the family moved to Hot Springs, Arkansas. There, Roger and Virginia had a son named Roger.

Billy's home life was hard. His stepfather drank too much and sometimes hurt Virginia. So in April 1962, Virginia divorced Roger. But later that summer, they remarried. Billy wanted to share his family's last name. So, he changed his last name from Blythe to Clinton. He also began to go by Bill.

A FUTURE LEADER

In Hot Springs, Bill attended Hot Springs High School. He was a busy student and a good musician. Bill played saxophone in the school band. He also competed in band festivals, where he won many medals. Every summer, Bill attended band camp in Fayetteville, Arkansas.

Bill considered President Kennedy his hero.

Bill also participated in student government. He belonged to the American Legion Boys Nation. This club is for students interested in government.

Bill visited Washington, D.C., with the Boys Nation in 1963. While there, he shook hands with President John F. Kennedy. Bill knew then that he wanted a life in politics.

Georgetown University sits on the banks of the Potomac River.

In 1964, Bill graduated from high school. Then he attended Georgetown University in Washington, D.C. There, Bill studied **political science** and world issues.

At Georgetown, Bill served as class president two years in a row. He also worked as an **intern** for Arkansas senator J. William Fulbright. In 1968, Bill graduated.

That fall, Bill began attending Oxford University in England. As a **Rhodes scholar**, he studied there for two years. Then, Bill traveled around Europe before returning to the United States.

LAW AND MARRIAGE

In 1970, Clinton went to Yale Law School in New Haven, Connecticut. In addition to studying, he worked as a lawyer's assistant. He also taught a law class at the

The Clintons at Yale

University of New Haven. Clinton graduated from Yale in 1973.

That spring, Clinton passed his examination to become a lawyer. Then he moved to Fayetteville, Arkansas. He took a job teaching at the University of Arkansas School of Law.

In 1974, Clinton ran for the U.S. House of Representatives. He lost the race, so he continued to teach law. Clinton also stayed interested in politics.

While at Yale, Clinton had met Hillary Diane Rodham. She had been a law student, too. Together, they had worked on **Democratic** senator George McGovern's 1972 presidential campaign. The two had grown close. They married on October 11, 1975. Eventually, the Clintons had a daughter. Chelsea was born in 1980.

Chelsea is Mr. and Mrs. Clinton's only child.

GOVERNOR CLINTON

In 1976, Clinton ran for Arkansas **attorney general** and won. He held this position for two years. Then in 1978, Clinton ran for governor of Arkansas. He won! The next year, Clinton became the youngest governor the country had seen in 40 years.

Governor Clinton had many ideas for new programs. He worked to improve schools, fix welfare, repair roads, and create jobs. To pay for these programs, Clinton raised taxes. This upset voters.

Clinton had other problems, too. He upset logging companies by saying they harvested too many Arkansas forests. Clinton also angered voters when thousands of Cuban **refugees** came to Arkansas. Their care cost taxpayers much money.

In 1980, Governor Clinton ran for reelection. Voters were still upset with him, so he did not win. After the election, Clinton returned to practicing law. He joined the firm of Wright, Lindsey, and Jennings in Little Rock, Arkansas.

As attorney general, Clinton supported the interests of consumers.

RETURN TO POLITICS

Clinton still wanted to work in politics. So, he ran for governor again in 1982. This time, he said he had learned from his mistakes. The voters believed him and voted him into office. Clinton went on to be reelected three more times.

Governor Clinton supported laws to improve education. Soon, teachers were tested to be sure they knew their subjects well. Parents received fines if they did not attend parent-teacher conferences. And, any student who quit school lost his or her driver's license.

Clinton announced his candidacy for president on October 3, 1991. He and Gore (left) were elected on November 3, 1992.

Governor Clinton improved the **economy**, too. He worked on laws that drew businesses to Arkansas. Soon, there were many well-paying jobs. Clinton also developed a new plan for welfare. It provided job training for those receiving welfare benefits.

Clinton was now known nationwide. So in 1992, the **Democratic** Party nominated him for president. Clinton chose Tennessee senator Al Gore as his **running mate**. **Republicans** renominated President George H.W. Bush and Vice President Dan Quayle.

President George H.W. Bush

Voters were upset with Bush because of the poor national economy. So, Clinton won the election! He earned 370 electoral votes, while Bush received only 168.

PRESIDENT CLINTON

Clinton took office on January 20, 1993. Congress soon passed many laws Clinton supported. The Brady Handgun Violence Prevention Act passed in 1993. This bill tightened gun control laws.

At Clinton's inauguration, he emphasized the importance of individuals taking responsibility to make the country a better place.

SUPREME COURT APPOINTMENTS

RUTH BADER GINSBURG - 1993
STEPHEN G. BREYER - 1994

President Clinton signed the Family and Medical Leave Act on February 5, 1993.

Another important law was the Family and Medical Leave Act. This allowed employees time off to care for a new baby or a sick family member.

Then in October, Clinton suggested ways to improve America's health care system. His plan would allow all Americans to get health **insurance**. However, Congress voted against Clinton's plan.

Clinton also worked on the North American Free Trade Agreement (NAFTA). It took effect on January 1, 1994. NAFTA slowly ended **tariffs** on goods exchanged between the United States, Mexico, and Canada. This greatly improved trade.

Clinton encouraged peace talks between Israeli prime minister Yitzhak Rabin (left) *and Palestine Liberation Organization chairman Yasir Arafat* (right).

President Clinton worked with other countries, too. In 1993, he had invited leaders from Israel and Palestine to sign a peace agreement. Then in 1994, Clinton sent U.S. troops to Haiti. They returned Haiti's president to power after he had been overthrown. In 1995, Clinton sent U.S. troops to Bosnia to help maintain peace.

Meanwhile, the Clintons faced personal problems. They had invested in some Arkansas property with the Whitewater Development Corporation. But, some people believed the land deals were illegal.

In 1994, the U.S. government hired lawyer Kenneth Starr to investigate the case. Clinton **testified** before Congress. His business partners were found guilty in May 1996. But, the charges against the Clintons were dropped. This **scandal** became known as the Whitewater affair.

That same year, President Clinton and Vice President Gore ran for reelection. The **Republican** Party nominated Senator Bob Dole of Kansas for president. Former congressman Jack Kemp became his **running mate**. Times were good, so voters did not want a change. Clinton easily won the election.

Dole (below) *received just 159 electoral votes to Clinton's 379.*

SECOND TERM

In 1999, the Clintons traveled to Europe. Clinton spoke to NATO troops helping with the conflict in Kosovo.

During Clinton's second term, America faced conflicts in other countries. In 1998, **terrorists** based in Afghanistan bombed U.S. **embassies** in Africa. Clinton ordered military attacks against the terrorists.

At the same time, Iraq would not let the **United Nations (UN)** inspect its weapons factories. The UN feared Iraq was making dangerous weapons. So, President Clinton ordered military attacks against Iraq.

Meanwhile, Yugoslavia had been attacking people in Kosovo. In March 1999, Clinton supported attacks on Yugoslavia by **NATO**. By June, Yugoslavia agreed to stop the fighting. So, NATO stopped its attacks. It also sent troops to Kosovo to keep the peace. About 7,000 American soldiers joined the effort.

PRESIDENT CLINTON'S CABINET

FIRST TERM
JANUARY 20, 1993– JANUARY 20, 1997

- **STATE** – Warren M. Christopher
- **TREASURY** – Lloyd Bentsen Jr.
  Robert E. Rubin (from January 10, 1995)
- **ATTORNEY GENERAL** – Janet Reno
- **INTERIOR** – Bruce Babbitt
- **AGRICULTURE** – Mike Espy
  Dan Glickman (from March 30, 1995)
- **COMMERCE** – Ronald H. Brown
  Mickey Kantor (from April 12, 1996)
- **LABOR** – Robert B. Reich
- **DEFENSE** – Les Aspin
  William J. Perry (from February 3, 1994)
- **HEALTH AND HUMAN SERVICES** –
  Donna E. Shalala
- **HOUSING AND URBAN DEVELOPMENT** –
  Henry G. Cisneros
- **TRANSPORTATION** – Federico Peña
- **ENERGY** – Hazel R. O'Leary
- **EDUCATION** – Richard W. Riley
- **VETERANS AFFAIRS** – Jesse Brown

SECOND TERM
JANUARY 20, 1997– JANUARY 20, 2001

- **STATE** – Madeleine Albright
- **TREASURY** – Robert E. Rubin
  Lawrence H. Summers (from July 2, 1999)
- **ATTORNEY GENERAL** – Janet Reno
- **INTERIOR** – Bruce Babbitt
- **AGRICULTURE** – Dan Glickman
- **COMMERCE** – William M. Daley
  Norman Mineta (from July 21, 2000)
- **LABOR** – Alexis M. Herman
- **DEFENSE** – William Cohen
- **HEALTH AND HUMAN SERVICES** –
  Donna E. Shalala
- **HOUSING AND URBAN DEVELOPMENT** –
  Andrew M. Cuomo
- **TRANSPORTATION** – Rodney Slater
- **ENERGY** – Federico Peña
  Bill Richardson (from August 18, 1998)
- **EDUCATION** – Richard W. Riley
- **VETERANS AFFAIRS** – Togo D. West Jr.
  Hershel W. Gober (from July 25, 2000)

Madeleine Albright

Bill Richardson

Back home, Clinton had named Madeleine Albright **secretary of state** in 1996. The next year, she became the first woman to head the Department of State. Clinton also named Bill Richardson as America's head delegate to the **UN**. Richardson was the first Hispanic to hold this job.

President Clinton continued working to decrease government spending. During this time, the **economy** continued to grow. For the first time since 1969, the government had a budget **surplus**. And by 1998, many more people had jobs and owned their own homes.

Meanwhile, Clinton had additional personal problems. Back in 1994, a woman named Paula Jones had filed a **lawsuit** against him. A judge threw out

Starr served as independent counsel while investigating Clinton. This type of lawyer helps trials that involve political parties remain fair.

the case in April 1998. However, Jones appealed the case. And, Kenneth Starr wanted to investigate Clinton further.

On August 17, 1998, Clinton appeared before a **grand jury**. He swore to tell the truth. Clinton then settled the Jones **lawsuit** in November. But his problems were not over.

IMPEACHMENT

Starr had sent a report to the U.S. House of Representatives in September. It said Clinton may have lied to the **grand jury**. Lying in court is a crime called perjury.

The House delivered this binder to the Senate. It contained the articles of impeachment. Clinton is only the second U.S. president to be impeached.

So in December 1998, the House of Representatives **impeached** Clinton. The House passed two articles of impeachment. One said Clinton may have committed perjury. The other said Clinton may have asked others to lie, too. This is called obstruction of justice.

Next, the U.S. Senate held a trial. They tried to figure out if Clinton was guilty of the two articles. They also tried to decide if Clinton should lose his job as president. On February 12, 1999, the Senate found Clinton not guilty. So, he was allowed to remain president.

Mrs. Clinton was elected a U.S. senator by the people of New York.

President Clinton continued to work hard after his **impeachment**. In early 2000, he supported a new law to improve trade with China. That same year, Clinton signed a trade agreement with Vietnam.

Clinton was also busy with the 2000 election. That year, he helped his wife become a U.S. senator. Clinton also helped Vice President Gore run for president. However, Gore lost the election to Texas governor George W. Bush.

MOVING ON

In January 2001, the Clintons left the White House and moved to New York. The next year, Clinton started the William J. Clinton Foundation. It addresses problems such as **AIDS**, poverty, and climate change.

In 2004, Clinton published his **autobiography** called *My Life*. That December, the William J. Clinton Presidential Center opened in Little Rock. It includes a library and a museum.

Clinton and former president George H.W. Bush joined efforts in 2005. Together, they worked to raise money for victims of natural

The William J. Clinton Presidential Center

disasters. Then in 2007, Clinton published the book *Giving: How Each of Us Can Change the World*.

That same year, Clinton's wife announced her candidacy for president. Clinton gave many speeches on her behalf. He hoped to help her win the **Democratic** nomination. Then in June 2008, Mrs. Clinton withdrew from the race to support Barack Obama.

During his presidency, Clinton worked hard to improve social problems and the **economy**. Today, Bill Clinton remains devoted to making the world a better place.

Clinton often travels to parts of the world where the Clinton Foundation offers support.

OFFICE OF THE PRESIDENT

BRANCHES OF GOVERNMENT

The U.S. government is divided into three branches. They are the executive, legislative, and judicial branches. This division is called a separation of powers. Each branch has some power over the others. This is called a system of checks and balances.

EXECUTIVE BRANCH

The executive branch enforces laws. It is made up of the president, the vice president, and the president's cabinet. The president represents the United States around the world. He or she oversees relations with other countries and signs treaties. The president signs bills into law and appoints officials and federal judges. He or she also leads the military and manages government workers.

LEGISLATIVE BRANCH

The legislative branch makes laws, maintains the military, and regulates trade. It also has the power to declare war. This branch consists of the Senate and the House of Representatives. Together, these two houses make up Congress. Each state has two senators. A state's population determines the number of representatives it has.

JUDICIAL BRANCH

The judicial branch interprets laws. It consists of district courts, courts of appeals, and the Supreme Court. District courts try cases. If a person disagrees with a trial's outcome, he or she may appeal. If the courts of appeals support the ruling, a person may appeal to the Supreme Court. The Supreme Court also makes sure that laws follow the U.S. Constitution.

QUALIFICATIONS FOR OFFICE

To be president, a person must meet three requirements. A candidate must be at least 35 years old and a natural-born U.S. citizen. He or she must also have lived in the United States for at least 14 years.

ELECTORAL COLLEGE

The U.S. presidential election is an indirect election. Voters from each state choose electors to represent them in the Electoral College. The number of electors from each state is based on population. Each elector has one electoral vote. Electors are pledged to cast their vote for the candidate who receives the highest number of popular votes in their state. A candidate must receive the majority of Electoral College votes to win.

TERM OF OFFICE

Each president may be elected to two four-year terms. Sometimes, a president may only be elected once. This happens if he or she served more than two years of the previous president's term.

The presidential election is held on the Tuesday after the first Monday in November. The president is sworn in on January 20 of the following year. At that time, he or she takes the oath of office:

I do solemnly swear (or affirm) that I will faithfully execute the office of President of the United States, and will to the best of my ability, preserve, protect and defend the Constitution of the United States.

Line of Succession

The Presidential Succession Act of 1947 defines who becomes president if the president cannot serve. The vice president is first in the line of succession. Next are the Speaker of the House and the President Pro Tempore of the Senate. If none of these individuals is able to serve, the office falls to the president's cabinet members. They would take office in the order in which each department was created:

Secretary of State

Secretary of the Treasury

Secretary of Defense

Attorney General

Secretary of the Interior

Secretary of Agriculture

Secretary of Commerce

Secretary of Labor

Secretary of Health and Human Services

Secretary of Housing and Urban Development

Secretary of Transportation

Secretary of Energy

Secretary of Education

Secretary of Veterans Affairs

Secretary of Homeland Security

BENEFITS

- While in office, the president receives a salary of $400,000 each year. He or she lives in the White House and has 24-hour Secret Service protection.

- The president may travel on a Boeing 747 jet called Air Force One. The airplane can accommodate 70 passengers. It has kitchens, a dining room, sleeping areas, and a conference room. It also has fully equipped offices with the latest communications systems. Air Force One can fly halfway around the world before needing to refuel. It can even refuel in flight!

- If the president wishes to travel by car, he or she uses Cadillac One. Cadillac One is a Cadillac Deville. It has been modified with heavy armor and communications systems. The president takes Cadillac One along when visiting other countries if secure transportation will be needed.

- The president also travels on a helicopter called Marine One. Like the presidential car, Marine One accompanies the president when traveling abroad if necessary.

- Sometimes, the president needs to get away and relax with family and friends. Camp David is the official presidential retreat. It is located in the cool, wooded mountains in Maryland. The U.S. Navy maintains the retreat, and the U.S. Marine Corps keeps it secure. The camp offers swimming, tennis, golf, and hiking.

- When the president leaves office, he or she receives Secret Service protection for ten more years. He or she also receives a yearly pension of $191,300 and funding for office space, supplies, and staff.

PRESIDENTS AND THEIR TERMS

PRESIDENT	PARTY	TOOK OFFICE	LEFT OFFICE	TERMS SERVED	VICE PRESIDENT
George Washington	None	April 30, 1789	March 4, 1797	Two	John Adams
John Adams	Federalist	March 4, 1797	March 4, 1801	One	Thomas Jefferson
Thomas Jefferson	Democratic-Republican	March 4, 1801	March 4, 1809	Two	Aaron Burr, George Clinton
James Madison	Democratic-Republican	March 4, 1809	March 4, 1817	Two	George Clinton, Elbridge Gerry
James Monroe	Democratic-Republican	March 4, 1817	March 4, 1825	Two	Daniel D. Tompkins
John Quincy Adams	Democratic-Republican	March 4, 1825	March 4, 1829	One	John C. Calhoun
Andrew Jackson	Democrat	March 4, 1829	March 4, 1837	Two	John C. Calhoun, Martin Van Buren
Martin Van Buren	Democrat	March 4, 1837	March 4, 1841	One	Richard M. Johnson
William H. Harrison	Whig	March 4, 1841	April 4, 1841	Died During First Term	John Tyler
John Tyler	Whig	April 6, 1841	March 4, 1845	Completed Harrison's Term	Office Vacant
James K. Polk	Democrat	March 4, 1845	March 4, 1849	One	George M. Dallas
Zachary Taylor	Whig	March 5, 1849	July 9, 1850	Died During First Term	Millard Fillmore

PRESIDENTS 1–12, 1789–1850

PRESIDENT	PARTY	TOOK OFFICE	LEFT OFFICE	TERMS SERVED	VICE PRESIDENT
Millard Fillmore	Whig	July 10, 1850	March 4, 1853	Completed Taylor's Term	Office Vacant
Franklin Pierce	Democrat	March 4, 1853	March 4, 1857	One	William R.D. King
James Buchanan	Democrat	March 4, 1857	March 4, 1861	One	John C. Breckinridge
Abraham Lincoln	Republican	March 4, 1861	April 15, 1865	Served One Term, Died During Second Term	Hannibal Hamlin, Andrew Johnson
Andrew Johnson	Democrat	April 15, 1865	March 4, 1869	Completed Lincoln's Second Term	Office Vacant
Ulysses S. Grant	Republican	March 4, 1869	March 4, 1877	Two	Schuyler Colfax, Henry Wilson
Rutherford B. Hayes	Republican	March 3, 1877	March 4, 1881	One	William A. Wheeler
James A. Garfield	Republican	March 4, 1881	September 19, 1881	Died During First Term	Chester Arthur
Chester Arthur	Republican	September 20, 1881	March 4, 1885	Completed Garfield's Term	Office Vacant
Grover Cleveland	Democrat	March 4, 1885	March 4, 1889	One	Thomas A. Hendricks
Benjamin Harrison	Republican	March 4, 1889	March 4, 1893	One	Levi P. Morton
Grover Cleveland	Democrat	March 4, 1893	March 4, 1897	One	Adlai E. Stevenson
William McKinley	Republican	March 4, 1897	September 14, 1901	Served One Term, Died During Second Term	Garret A. Hobart, Theodore Roosevelt

PRESIDENT	PARTY	TOOK OFFICE	LEFT OFFICE	TERMS SERVED	VICE PRESIDENT
Theodore Roosevelt	Republican	September 14, 1901	March 4, 1909	Completed McKinley's Second Term, Served One Term	Office Vacant, Charles Fairbanks
William Taft	Republican	March 4, 1909	March 4, 1913	One	James S. Sherman
Woodrow Wilson	Democrat	March 4, 1913	March 4, 1921	Two	Thomas R. Marshall
Warren G. Harding	Republican	March 4, 1921	August 2, 1923	Died During First Term	Calvin Coolidge
Calvin Coolidge	Republican	August 3, 1923	March 4, 1929	Completed Harding's Term, Served One Term	Office Vacant, Charles Dawes
Herbert Hoover	Republican	March 4, 1929	March 4, 1933	One	Charles Curtis
Franklin D. Roosevelt	Democrat	March 4, 1933	April 12, 1945	Served Three Terms, Died During Fourth Term	John Nance Garner, Henry A. Wallace, Harry S. Truman
Harry S. Truman	Democrat	April 12, 1945	January 20, 1953	Completed Roosevelt's Fourth Term, Served One Term	Office Vacant, Alben Barkley
Dwight D. Eisenhower	Republican	January 20, 1953	January 20, 1961	Two	Richard Nixon
John F. Kennedy	Democrat	January 20, 1961	November 22, 1963	Died During First Term	Lyndon B. Johnson
Lyndon B. Johnson	Democrat	November 22, 1963	January 20, 1969	Completed Kennedy's Term, Served One Term	Office Vacant, Hubert H. Humphrey
Richard Nixon	Republican	January 20, 1969	August 9, 1974	Completed First Term, Resigned During Second Term	Spiro T. Agnew, Gerald Ford

PRESIDENT	PARTY	TOOK OFFICE	LEFT OFFICE	TERMS SERVED	VICE PRESIDENT
Gerald Ford	Republican	August 9, 1974	January 20, 1977	Completed Nixon's Second Term	Nelson A. Rockefeller
Jimmy Carter	Democrat	January 20, 1977	January 20, 1981	One	Walter Mondale
Ronald Reagan	Republican	January 20, 1981	January 20, 1989	Two	George H.W. Bush
George H.W. Bush	Republican	January 20, 1989	January 20, 1993	One	Dan Quayle
Bill Clinton	Democrat	January 20, 1993	January 20, 2001	Two	Al Gore
George W. Bush	Republican	January 20, 2001	January 20, 2009	Two	Dick Cheney
Barack Obama	Democrat	January 20, 2009			Joe Biden

"There is nothing wrong with America that cannot be cured by what is right with America." Bill Clinton

WRITE TO THE PRESIDENT

You may write to the president at:

**The White House
1600 Pennsylvania Avenue NW
Washington, DC 20500**

You may e-mail the president at:

comments@whitehouse.gov

GLOSSARY

AIDS - Acquired Immune Deficiency Syndrome. A disease that weakens the
immune system. It is caused by the Human Immunodeficiency Virus (HIV).

attorney general - the chief law officer of a national or state government.

autobiography - a story of a person's life that is written by himself or herself.

Democrat - a member of the Democratic political party. Democrats believe in
social change and strong government.

disaster - a sudden event that causes destruction and suffering or loss of life.
Natural disasters include events such as hurricanes, tornadoes, and
earthquakes.

economy - the way a nation uses its money, goods, and natural resources.

embassy - the home and office of a diplomat who lives in a foreign country.

grand jury - a group of people who investigate a crime. The group decides if
there is enough evidence for a trial.

impeach - to charge a public official with misconduct in office.

insurance - a contract that helps people pay their bills if they are sick or hurt.
People with insurance pay money each month to keep the contract.

intern - an advanced student or graduate gaining supervised practical experience
in his or her field. A person doing this is participating in an internship.

lawsuit - a case held before a court.

NATO - North Atlantic Treaty Organization. A group formed by the United
States, Canada, and some European countries in 1949. It tries to create
peace among its nations and protect them from common enemies.

political science - the study of government and politics.

refugee - a person who flees to another country for safety and protection.

Republican - a member of the Republican political party. Republicans are conservative and believe in small government.

Rhodes scholar - a student who has a scholarship to Oxford University. It is given to students with good grades who have shown leadership.

running mate - a candidate running for a lower-rank position on an election ticket, especially the candidate for vice president.

scandal - an action that shocks people and disgraces those connected with it.

secretary of state - a member of the president's cabinet who handles relations with other countries.

surplus - an amount above what is needed.

tariff - the taxes a government puts on imported or exported goods.

terrorist - a person who uses violence to threaten people or governments.

testify - to speak under oath in a court of law.

United Nations (UN) - a group of nations formed in 1945. Its goals are peace, human rights, security, and social and economic development.

WEB SITES

To learn more about Bill Clinton, visit ABDO Publishing Company on the World Wide Web at **www.abdopublishing.com**. Web sites about Bill Clinton are featured on our Book Links page. These links are routinely monitored and updated to provide the most current information available.

INDEX